We Are All Unique And Meaningful To This World

By Anise Marshall   Illustrated by Jasmine Hatcher

5 Royal Sisters Publishing, LLC

The Sister Keepers™

book series

5 Royal Sisters
PUBLISHING, LLC

Text used: Bradley Hand, Eurostile, Comic Sans MS, Gabriola pink and Ayuthaya

Cover and Illustrations by Jasmine Hatcher

www.thesisterkeepers.com

The Sister Keepers ™ book series

ISBN-13: 978-1-7320621-0-8

THE SISTER KEEPERS BOOK SERIES WAS WRITTEN TO ENCOURAGE YOUTH, PROMOTE AWARENESS FOR CHILDREN WITH DISABILITIES, PROMOTE KINDNESS, ENCOURAGE CONFLICT RESOLUTION, MAKE EVERLASTING FRIENDSHIPS AND STAND UP AGAINST BULLYING. 5 ROYAL SISTERS PUBLISHING, LLC IS ALL ABOUT BEING THE BEST VERSION OF YOURSELF. I DEDICATE THIS BOOK TO MY DAUGHTERS AND TO ALL OF THE CHILDREN WHO FEEL INSPIRED TO CHANGE THE WORLD, ONE DAY AT A TIME.

THANK YOU, ANISE MARSHALL

Daddy, I don't want her to come to my room!

I am 3 years older than her. She can barely read!

2

You are correct,
Shanise! She can
"barely" read. But,
today, you will
show her how to
become a better
reader!

Daddy, NO....

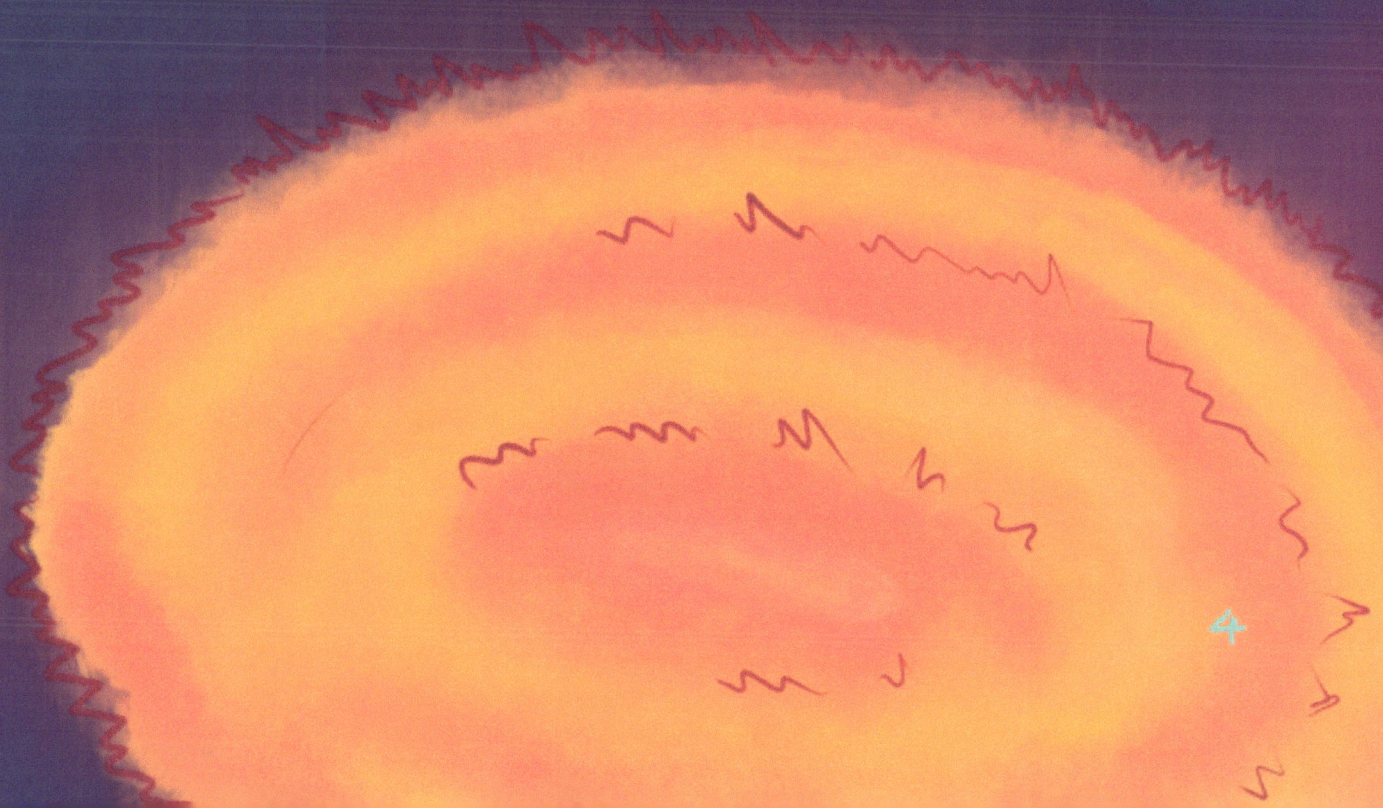

4

Alysse, I don't know why you're laughing! You will teach Alyssa how to draw!

Daddy, that's not fair!

HA, I knew it! Alysse, you have to show me something NEW!

6

I want to draw a
ballerina...in a
tutu singing...into a
microphone!

Good idea, Alyssa!

When you're done, you
can teach Alana how to
sing her favorite song!

Yes!

I love you, Alyssa

I've always wanted to sing!

You're a really good singer, too!

Would you teach me that

new song by Natalia?

Daddy, since I'm Alana, the BIG girl, I can show Shannon how to color in the lines!

That's a really good idea, Alana!

That is how you treat a sister!

12

Good job, Alysse! I'm proud of you!

Now, always sound like you're shushing someone when you put the letter 's' and 'n' together. It's just like my name.

SH-A-NISE.

14

15

Alyssa, you have to take

your time.

Push lightly on the pencil
to shade. Those
instructions will help you
when you start on the

tutu.

Alana, this song is in a different language. It's going to be hard at first, but you will get the hang of it. Listen to the words.

Take your time when the notes change. Say "mi Dios es asombroso." That means,

God is Amazing.

¡Mi Dios es asombroso!

Did I say it right, Alyssa

Yes, you said it perfect, Alana!

Shannon, if you trace the line on the picture, it will help you stay inside the lines.

Learn from one another.

No one knows everything!

    I need each one

of you to know that you are

unique in your OWN way!

You mean something to this

      World!

How you deal

with conflict,

prepares you for

lasting

    friendships.

24

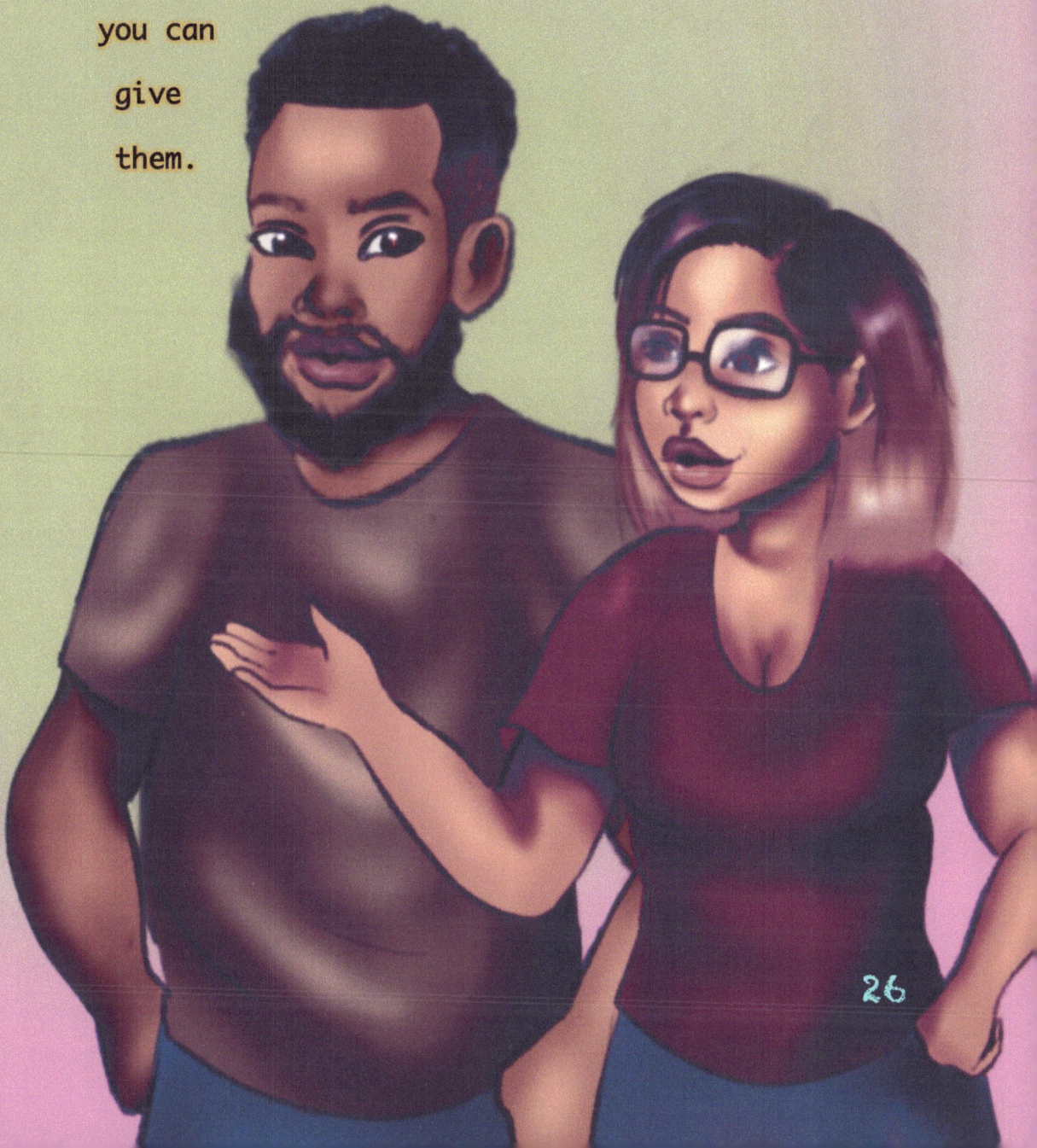

Ladies, settle down! Your sisters are your first friends.

Teach someone something new and it will stick with them forever.

It is the best gift

you can

 give

 them.

I love all the beautiful

sketches!

We will call you
"The Sister Keepers"
from now on!

You ALL

have something

unique to add to our mural!

Would anyone like a
frozen mango and
chamoy smoothie?

WAIT, HAS ANYONE
SEEN SHANNON?

What is Shannon
doing?

She has on a cape!

She looks like a
superhero!

How did she get there so fast?

She IS a superhero!

I bet, she will do
amazing things!

ABOUT THE AUTHOR:

Anise Marshall is the owner of 5 Royal Sisters Publishing and the Author of the book series: "The Sister Keepers." Anise was a managing editor for an amazing magazine and a teacher for 2 years. She has a bachelor's degree in journalism and Advertising with a minor in English as well as, a master's degree in Curriculum and Instruction with a concentration in teacher leadership. Anise can be found at WWW.THESISTERKEEPERS.COM where she has monthly blogs for mothers and bonding challenges for little girls and their moms! She is dedicated to changing the future of our youth. She does speaking engagements and educates schools and communities about the importance of pulling out the creativity in every child!

33

www.ingramcontent.com/pod-product-compliance
Lightning Source LLC
LaVergne TN
LVHW072056070426
835508LV00002B/118